STILL MARRIED AFTER ALL THESE YEARS

Illustrated by
Renée Williams

The recreational activity you most often do together is:

A) Bicycling.   B) Bowling.

C) Hunting for his car keys.

3

A) Simply a tube of toothpaste squeezed in the middle.

B) Proof that "some people" could care less about other people's feelings and always have to get their way.

CHOOSE A VACATION SPOT!

Which qualifications for a prime vacation spot would appeal to the husband, and which would appeal to the wife?

1) Quaint, little shops.
2) Golf, golf, golf.
3) Nice restaurants.
4) Big servings.
5) Valet parking.
6) Free parking.
7) Room with a view.
8) Room with a TV.
9) Elegant sunken tub.
10) Reading matter in bathroom.

Wife   Husband

5

WHAT DOES THIS LOOK LIKE TO YOU?

A) The molecular structure of Xyenon.

B) Two bunches of grapes, plus one that has rolled away.

C) Top view of you at your spouse's office party.

A bunch of burly bruisers who chain-smoke and swill beer are coming over to play cards and grind hoagie sandwiches into your carpet. You can't help but think:

A) I hope they have fun.

B) Sometimes sacrifices are necessary in a marriage.

C) My wife knows some tough women!

When you see your husband with his shirt off, you are most likely to say:

A) "What cute little love handles!"

B) "There's more of you to love!"

C) "Thar she blows!"

When you see your wife in a swimsuit, you are most likely to say:

A) "You look great!"

B) "You look wonderful!"

C) "You look fantastic!"

TRUE OR FALSE: A vacuum cleaner makes an excellent anniversary gift.

TRUE! Provided you want it to be your last anniversary.

STORY PROBLEM:

John and Betty must leave their home by 6 p.m. in order to be on time for a dinner party. John starts to get ready at 5:55, so he can leave at 6. What time does Betty need to start getting ready in order to leave by 6 ?

ANSWER: It makes no difference when Betty starts to get ready. She could start at 5 p.m., 4 p.m., or even 3 p.m. It doesn't matter. She's still going to be at least 20 minutes late.

11

When your wife says "Let's not get each other Christmas presents this year," it indicates:

A) Her desire to share with the less fortunate.

B) Her thoughtful and realistic interest in the household budget.

C) A test to see if you "love her enough" to forget the suggestion and "surprise" her with something you'll be paying off until Columbus Day.

When a husband dons his almost-like-new coveralls and announces, "I'm going to work on the car", you can almost bet that:

A) Soon, it will purr like a kitten.
B) Soon, it will stop on a dime.
C) Soon, it will be towed to a nearby garage.

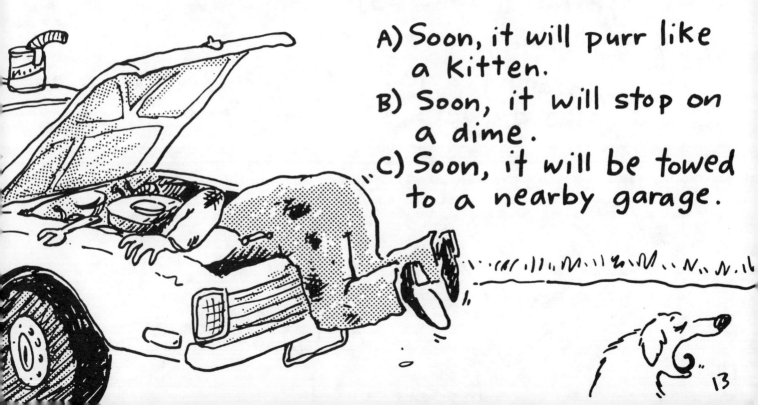

13

FILL IN THE BLANK:

You can't make an omelet without _____

    A) Breaking some eggs.

    B) Reading a recipe.

    C) Hearing a lecture from your wife on the dangers of cholesterol.

THIS IS A DRAWING OF:

A) The cross section of a technical blueprint.

B) The lever system of a movable bridge.

C) The back wall of the garage just before a big fight.

When you hear the classic rock song, "You Can't Always Get What You Want", you think of :

A) A new car.

B) A bigger house

C) The TV remote control.

A fun maze for you to work together! Husbands, steer your wife past the distractions to the <u>one</u> thing you came to the mall to buy.

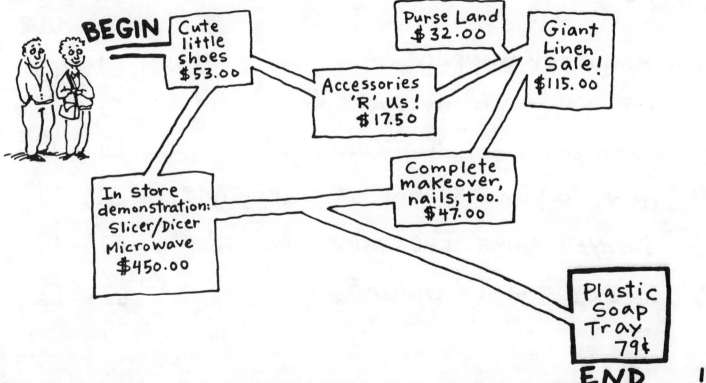

WHO IS MORE LIKELY TO UTTER THE FOLLOWING?

	HIM	HER
1. "What's for supper?"	☐	☐
2. "Have you seen my socks?"	☐	☐
3. "When are we going dancing?"	☐	☐
4. "How do you like my new hairstyle?"	☐	☐
5. "Do you think I've gained weight?"	☐	☐
6. "Where's the TV Guide?"	☐	☐

Nothing is certain in life but death and _____.

      A) Taxes.

      B) Disappointment.

      C) A husband retelling the same joke over and over at a party.

Before answering the question "How do you like my new hairstyle?" what should a husband always remember?

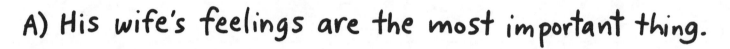

A) His wife's feelings are the most important thing.

B) She may have spent hours in a salon to get it to look that way.

C) The couch is lumpy, and when you sleep on it a spring pokes you in the back.

NAME THIS PICTURE:

A) Ants descending on a vanilla wafer.

B) The Milky Way Galaxy.

C) The bathroom sink after your husband shaves.

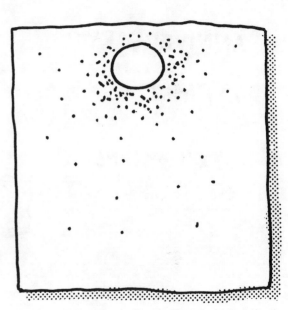

MATCH THE ANNIVERSARY AT LEFT WITH THE SLEEPWEAR AT RIGHT.

ANNIVERSARY:

A) First.

B) All others.

SLEEPWEAR:

a) HERS: Sexy, see-through nightie.
HIS: Nothing.

b) HERS: Flannel nightgown.
HIS: T-shirt, boxer shorts.

HIS IDEA OF THE PERFECT SECOND HONEYMOON IS:

A) A week in the Poconos.

B) A Mediterranean cruise.

C) Anything under a hundred bucks.

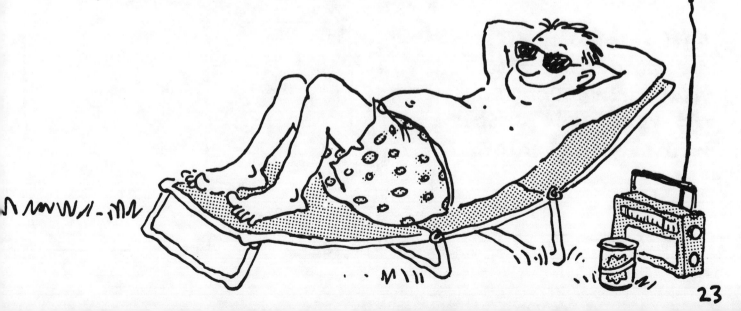

The phrase "not in your lifetime" refers to:

A) Him cleaning the bathroom.

B) Her cleaning out the gutters.

C) Either of you ever cleaning that stuff that grows under the vegetable crisper in the refrigerator.

Here are charts showing how two people divide their time. Which is the husband's and which is the wife's?

Watching TV

Reading romance novels

Barbecuing

Waiting for wife in front of "cute little boutiques"

Shopping

picking up husbands dirty underwear

When you think about the love letters you used to write when you were courting, you're reminded:

A) Of a passion that burned like ancient Rome.

B) Of a love that will last for eternity.

C) That you're fortunate "corny" is not a crime.

What does the following clock position mean to you?

A) It's almost time to get up.

B) It's almost time for dinner.

C) There's just enough time for romance before the 6 o'clock news.

Often men and women will show the subtle signs of stress and strain in different ways. For each way listed below, circle the most appropriate gender.

1) Punch inanimate object, such as door or steering wheel.   M F Either

2) Make sniffling noises and sigh heavily.   M F Either

3) Blame clubs, bat, etc. for poor athletic performance.   M F Either

4) Clamp hands over face and weep. When questioned, Keep saying "Oh, nothing", over and over.   M F Either

When attending a formal party, it is best for the husband to wear:

A) A dark suit.

B) A tuxedo.

C) Whatever his wife picks out.

When the waiter asks what you'd like for dessert, a wife's most common response is:

A) "Chocolate mousse, please".

B) "I'll try the cheesecake."

C) "Oh, nothing for me. I'll just have a teensie bite of his."

OPTICAL ILLUSION:

Which couch is longer?

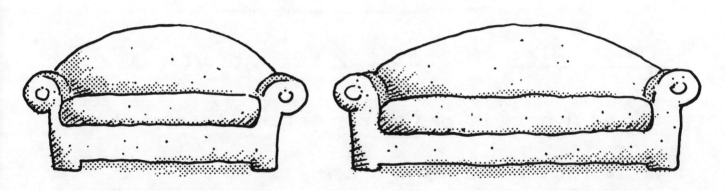

ANSWER: Whichever one your wife wants moved.

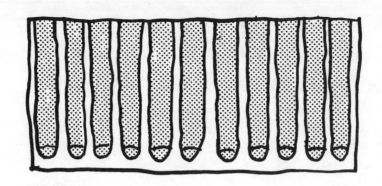

What does this object remind you of?

A) A pack of ordinary kitchen matches.

B) An open sardine can.

C) Pantyhose hanging over your bathtub.

Your husband tries on his high school letter jacket and finds he can no longer snap it up. A wife's best response is:

A) "Maybe it shrunk."

B) "I like you a little less skinny."

C) "That jacket would look dumb on a bald guy anyway."

What's wrong with this picture?

Answer: A husband is consulting a road map to see if he's really lost.

Some household chores are traditionally done by the man, some by the woman. Place the following chores in the correct category.

IS   HERS

1) Cooking.

2) Flattening couch cushions.

3) Cleaning.

4) Tossing newspaper sections around.

5) Dusting.

6) Snoring on Saturday afternoons.

Your spouse is snoring. Should you:

A) Accept it as a minor flaw in an otherwise perfect mate.

B) Gently nudge him and say "Roll over, dear."

C) Put a pair of sweatpants over his head and tighten the drawstring.

Who wants which addition to the house?

1) A cozy breakfast nook. Wife? Husband?

2) A red velour wallpapered den with big leather couches and a pinball machine and a pool/snooker table and a moose head and a telephone that looks like a football helmet and a huge-screen TV and stereo with tapes of every college basketball game ever played and a train set and... Wife? Husband?

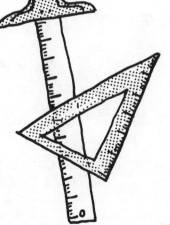

37

When riding with your husband on long car trips, you use the hours of quiet time to:

A) Discuss meaningful topics.

B) Point out the beauty of the scenery.

C) Excitedly warn him of impending highway danger that you can barely see as a tiny speck on the horizon.

If a longtime married couple
is in the bathtub together,
it can only mean:

a) They still feel passionately
   about each other.

b) Their love life is
   spontaneous and exciting.

c) He's grouting some
   loose tile while
   she tries to get
   rid of stubborn
   soap scum.

39

TRUE or FALSE: The husband often lets his wife answer the phone because it's usually for her anyway.

FALSE! The husband often lets his wife answer the phone because, if he doesn't, he may end up talking to her mother.

40

This glass is:

A) Half full.

B) Half empty.

c) Trouble, because there's no coaster under it.

41

A left to the head!

A right to the breadbasket!

A pair of kicks!

A flurry of jabs!

The action described above is probably:

A) A kickboxing match.

B) A scene from an action-adventure movie.

C) How one of you ends up with all the covers.

42

STORY PROBLEM:
If you had $100 in a joint bank account and wrote three checks for $10 each, how much would you have left?

ANSWER: Trick question! What about those three checks for odd amounts somebody forgot to post when she went to the mall last week?

43

What does the following ink blot look like to you ?

A) An apple.

B) A butterfly.

C) A spot on your husband's white shirt after he checks the oil in the car.

44

Occasionally, for various reasons, your spouse will be called away for a few days. During these times, you are most likely to:

A) Give the house a thorough cleaning.

B) Plan a surprise for your spouse's return.

C) Dirty every dish in the house, and clean them five minutes before your spouse gets home.

The phrase most often heard when the two of you are alone in a quiet setting is:

A) "I love you"

B) "I need you"

C) "Zzzzzzz..."

46

When entertaining another couple in your home, your biggest concern is:

A) That they feel comfortable.

B) That there is plenty of well-prepared food.

C) That they don't accidentally use the bathroom you didn't clean.

47

WHO IS MOST LIKELY TO READ WHICH BOOK?

	Him	Her
1) The Babe Ruth Story	☐	☐
2) Love's Bitter Fruit	☐	☐
3) The Stan (The Man) Musial Story	☐	☐
4) Love's Sweet Passion	☐	☐
5) The Joe DiMaggio Story	☐	☐
6) Love's Stormy Coastline	☐	☐
7) The Satchel Paige Story	☐	☐
8) Love's Trembling Upper Lip	☐	☐
9) The Abner Doubleday Story	☐	☐
10) Love's Loving Lovers	☐	☐

Arguing over which side of the roll the toilet paper should hang from is silly because:

A) It doesn't really matter.

B) Compromise is more important than winning.

C) It takes up valuable time that could be spent arguing whether to sleep with the window up or down.

What do you see in this picture?

A) True love.

B) Communication.

c) What?! No TV?!

Which of the following car options is your husband most likely to consider frivolous?

A) AM/FM Cassette.

B) Power seats.

C) Power sunroof.

D) All of the above! All that extra stuff will just break anyway! Geez...all you need is four tires and a good engine. You think those fancy cars get there any sooner?

What does this drawing probably represent?

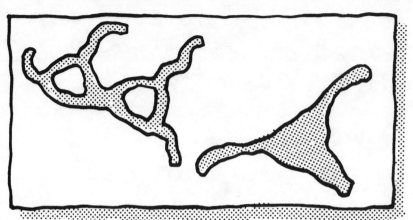

A) A group of islands in the Pacific.

B) A traditional Kabuki theater mask.

C) A husband's idea of comfortable sleepwear for the wife.

WHO WANTS WHICH PET?

cute, little puppy the size f a hefty gerbil that has bark only other dogs can ear, and a tendency towards ows in its fur and itty-bitty nit plaid sweaters. Probable ame: Mr. Poochie.

A dog that can chew cinder blocks in half and is never so happy as when standing tall in the back of a speeding pickup truck. Probable name: Conan.

lusband ☐   Wife ☐

Husband ☐   Wife ☐

FILL IN THE BLANK:

Early to bed and early to rise makes a man _____.

A) Irritable.

B) Healthy, wealthy and wise.

C) Have a better chance of sneaking out of the house with his golf bag.

Cleaning fish in the kitchen sink is a good way to:

A) Learn about the internal workings of the fish.

B) Act out a big "fish rumble" with a couple of them in each hand and lots of deep-voiced name-calling and squeaky-voiced cries for help.

C) End a marriage on the spot.

57

MATCH THE SOCK ON THE LEFT WITH THE CORRESPONDING SOCK ON THE RIGHT.

SCORING: If it took you:

- 1-5 seconds, you're a wife.

- 30-60 seconds, you're a small child.

- 1-2 hours, and even then you're not sure, you're a husband.

While enjoying a lazy weekend together, you probably find it easier to finish:

A) A sumptuous brunch.

B) The Sunday paper.

C) Each other's sentences.

A RIDDLE:

Which is more upsetting: Having a poorly dressed jerk operating heavy equipment in the yard slice through the telephone cable? Or having him slice through the TV cable?

Answer: Trick question! Most upsetting is realizing you married the jerk in the first place.

A husband offers to run to the store for a quart of milk. He is most likely to return with:

A) A quart of milk.

B) Two steaks, a big fish, a dozen cans of sardines in mustard sauce, two six-packs of beer, a box of donuts, a TV dinner, some head cheese, the latest issue of <u>Sports Monthly</u>, and a can of 40-weight motor oil.

C) A dazed expression and the question, "What was I supposed to get?"

Match the following statements with the correct response:

A) "Honey, would you take out the trash?"

a) "Yes, Dear."

B) "Stand up straight, Dear."

b) "Yes, Dear."

C) "Honey, could you help me with the dishes?"

c) "Yes, Dear."

D) "I like the red one better. Don't you like the red one better?"

d) "Yes, Dear."

To prove your love for your wife, you would gladly:

A) Climb the highest mountain.

B) Swim the deepest ocean.

C) Hold her purse while she tried things on at the mall and run the risk that, at any moment, one of the guys might walk by.

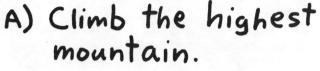

To prove your love for your husband, you would gladly:

A) Climb the highest mountain.

B) Swim the deepest ocean.

C) Put gas in the car at one of those self-serve places where the risk of a broken fingernail is a constant threat.

MATCH THE SYMPTOMS ON THE LEFT WITH THE APPROPRIATE VIRUS ON THE RIGHT.

) Pretty much does everything normally, stopping occasionally to sneeze or cough.

1) His cold.

) Takes three days off work, keeps croaking from another room for more warm toast, buys a $300 juicer to squeeze oranges and gets 15 bottles of over-the-counter medicine that remain unopened.

2) Her cold.

65

Match the husband's do-it-yourself project on the left with the correct solution on the right.

A) Replace gutters.

B) Install new sink.

c) Re-tile bathroom floor.

A) Call repairman.

B) Call repairman

C) Call repairman

66.

You enjoy going to parties with your spouse because:

A) Having common friends deepens your relationship.

B) You really enjoy seeing your mate have a good time.

C) Somebody else gets stuck cleaning the cheese dip out of the carpet for a change.

Choosing a rental video for an evening's entertainment c[an]
be difficult for some couples. Test your skill by match[-]
ing which spouse would probably prefer which movie belo[w]

1) Two People in Love: Two people meet and fall in love and say really sensitive things to each other.

2) Die Slowly: Half-naked women meet bully cops and defeat a ton of guys in really neat ways.

A) Husband.   B) Wife.

ROMANCE

AC

A) A man with a very large nose.

B) A two-celled amoeba.

C) The position of the bathroom seat after your husband uses it.

You're pleased that you had an extensive photo album made at your wedding because:

A) It's a joy to frequently gaze at the photos together.

B) It will be a valuable keepsake for your children.

C) You would have just squandered that thousand dollars on rent or food anyway.

You two will love each other:

A) Until the mountains crumble.

B) Until the stars fall from the sky.

C) Until she stops using your razor and "forgets" to tell you about it.

Other books from
SHOEBOX GREETINGS
(A tiny little division of Hallmark)

HEY GUY, ARE YOU: A) Getting Older? B) Getting Better? C) Getting Balder?
FRISKY BUSINESS: All About Being Owned by a Cat.
THE WORLD ACCORDING TO DENISE.
GIRLS JUST WANNA HAVE FACE LIFTS: The Ugly Truth About Getting Older.
DON'T WORRY, BE CRABBY: Maxine's Guide to Life.
EVERYTHING YOU ALWAYS WANTED TO KNOW ABOUT STRESS...but were too nervous, tense, irritable and moody to ask.
40: THE YEAR OF NAPPING DANGEROUSLY.
RAIDERS OF THE LOST BARK: A Collection of Canine Cartoons.
THE MOM DICTIONARY.
THE DAD DICTIONARY.
WAKE UP AND SMELL THE FORMULA: The A to No ZZZZ's of Having a Baby.
WORKIN' NOON TO FIVE: The Official Workplace Quizbook.
THE OFFICIAL COLLEGE QUIZ BOOK.
WHAT...ME, 30?
YOU EXPECT ME TO SWALLOW THAT?: The Official Hospital Quiz Book.
THE GOOD, THE PLAID, AND THE BOGEY: A Glossary of Golfing Terms.
THE COLLEGE DICTIONARY: A Book You'll Actually Read!
THE FISHING DICTIONARY: Everything You'll Say About the One That Got Away.